WHA[
DID [

OTHER BOOKS IN THIS SERIES

Dedication

This book is dedicated to the memory of Arnold McLay, undoubtedly one of the world's most brilliant and dedicated collectors of ornithological dejecta.

Arnold passed away in August 1986 while attempting to bring to our headquarters a rare triple splay of the Wryneck *(Jynx torquilla)*, which he had managed to collect on his windshield, some two hundred miles away in Dunbar. Unfortunately, the splay had almost completely obscured his vision and in order to see properly, Arnold was forced to drive with his head protruding from the driver's window. Tragically, he was only five miles from his destination when the combined effects of exhaustion and excitement caused him to misjudge the proximity of an oncoming truck and trailer.

His decapitation, however, was not in vain. Arnold's windshield and its remarkable splay miraculously survived the collision. It is, thankfully, preserved to this very day in the executive boardroom of the Birmingham Ornithological Dejecta Society.

In keeping with Arnold McLay's unswerving devotion to the preservation and study of splays, a commemorative plaque underneath the windshield simply reads:

> *"The Last Great Splay*
> *of Arnold McLay"*

Those words and that windshield are an inspiration to us all.

A constellation of Hairy Woodpecker *Picodes villosus* splays, The Bartle Collection.

WHAT BIRD DID THAT?

A driver's guide to some common birds of North America.

PETER HANSARD/BURTON SILVER

Ten Speed Press

Ten Speed Press
P.O. Box 7123 Berkeley, California 94707

First U.S. edition, 1991

Originated and devised by Peter Hansard and Burton Silver

Book design and production by Trevor Plaisted, Wellington

Typeset by Megbyte Graphics, Wellington

Cover photograph by Annelies Van Der Poel

Photographs © 1991 Burton Silver

Compiled by Silverculture Press
487 Karaka Bay Road, Wellington 3, New Zealand

Library of Congress Cataloging-in-Publication Data

Hansard, Peter.
What Bird Did that? : a driver's guide to some common birds of
    North America/Peter Hansard, Burton Silver.
        p.   cm.
ISBN 0-89815-427-8
1. Birds — North America — Identification. 2. Bird
droppings — North America — Identification. 3. Bird
droppings — Identification 4. Bird droppings — Pictorial
works. 5. Bird droppings — Humor. 6. Birds — Humor.
I. Silver, Burton. II. Title.
QL681.H26 1991
598.297 — dc20

                                        91 - 14292
                                            CIP

Printed in Hong Kong.

3 4 5 — 95 94

"I have always believed that birds do it quite without malice, indeed almost unconsciously, and certainly without any idea of the result. Were I to think otherwise, I would probably find it necessary to worship them. As it is I feel only a slight envy. Owls however, are quite a different matter."

Coots Na Hoot
Sir David McGill

Foreword

The noise of a bird dropping hitting a windshield at fifty miles an hour is usually soft, muted, almost ethereal. But this one sounded like a rifle-shot. We all jumped, shaken from our silent reveries first by the sharp crack and then by the marvel of colors and textures that spread slowly upwards before us.

With a skill born of great experience and dedication, the driver gradually slowed the car, so that now the fluids, previously held up as a bright quivering mass by the pressure of air, began to relax and glide gently downwards, spreading hues of green, crimson, white and gold in a myriad of vivid tentacles. When we finally stopped half a mile further on, at least a third of the windshield was covered with a most magnificent splay.

There are times in one's life which are visually memorable, and other times which are intellectually memorable, but seldom, except in the greatest of films and theatre are they ever perfectly combined. Yet this was to be such a time, for I was privileged to be sitting with Peter Hansard and Burton Silver, the world's leading experts in ornithological dejecta, while on a trip in the USA. And just inches away on the windshield, was one of the freshest, rarest and most beautiful of all splays.

It was Burton who broke the silence. *"Gallinula chloropus? Porphyrula martinica?"* he suggested tentatively.

"Yes, I can follow your thinking on that. Look, hardly any loss of opacity, greenish-brown and virtually no envelope. But we were doing at least fifty miles an hour and a gallinule splay would have strung itself out a bit more, don't you think?"

"Maybe, but if you're talking *Anas* as I think you are, then it's rather smaller than one would expect from a mallard and anyway, how do you explain this crimson tinge here?"

"Quite possibly marsh berries — I know it's a bit late for them but it is consistent with color and see here, this seems to be a seed casing."

"Hmm, could be insectivorous. Exoskeletal maybe. I still think a small coot or a gallinule, and perhaps a meal of marshberries swallowed whole with a small pebble. Or what about something like *Charadrius vociferus* feeding on contaminated earthworms? A piece of shell would account for the noise and a diseased soil animal would be consistent with this color."

This fascinating discussion continued for at least fifteen minutes before they eventually agreed, by a logical process of elimination, on the Blue-Winged Teal, *(Anas discors)*, with a displaced gizzard stone. Naturally, it was crucial to record this very rare splay, but they were out of film and it meant a further ten-mile drive to the next town before they could load up, take some shots and then carefully scrape the splay off for later analysis. They drove the ten miles in great excitement and were able to purchase film from a gas station.

We were all standing round the open trunk watching Peter load the camera when it happened. A gas station attendant casually strolled over and simply cleaned the splay right off with a rubber squeegee before anyone realized what he was doing.

Now I have to say, most people would have gone berserk, screamed and yelled, threatened legal action for tampering with private property, or whatever. But not these two. No, they've just had their most significant find in years destroyed, the Dead Sea Scrolls of ornithological dejecta wiped out - and what did they do? They very calmly took that young man aside and patiently explained to him what it was he had just done. He sat and listened and like me, he became enthralled. When we drove off two hours later, he was a changed man.

Peter Hansard and Burton Silver have dedicated the last three years to the compilation of this comprehensive field guide, pooling their vast experience and knowledge so that many more of us may have the chance to become captivated by the nuances of the splay and gain a greater understanding of our feathered friends. It is a tribute to their devotion and vision that the aforementioned attendant is now president of the National Ornithological Dejecta Society of America and boasts a personal collection of over three thousand splays, including two of the Blue-winged Teal.

Dr Peter Twite

Contents

SPLAY TOPOGRAPHY

A knowledge of the different parts of each splay is essential to fully describe and understand the variations in ornithological dejecta. The diagrams below show all the main areas of a splay as well as the main types of splay that the collector can expect to find.
(See also Glossary of Terms.)

Sub-nucleus
Nucleus
Solids
Envelope
Outer envelope
Inner envelope
Lobe
Detached lobe
Extended lobe
Sub-nuclear particles

Splerd

Large. Envelope covers greater area than the nucleus which may be almost non-existent. Little distinction between outer and inner envelopes.

Sklop

Small. Clearly defined envelope and nucleus of roughly equal proportions. No tendency to lobe. Usually taken at low speeds or results from short drop height.

Splood

Varies in size. Typified by a single extended lobe which may contain sub-nuclear particles and occasionally solids.

Schplutz

Varies in size with multiple extended lobes. The lower ones may contain sub-nuclear particles and the occasional solid.

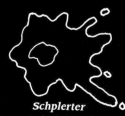

Schplerter

Large. Multiple extended and detached lobes. Usually taken at high speeds or results from extended drop height. Often has disintegrated nucleus.

Preface

There has long been a need, not only among the motoring public, but also with an ever increasing number of bird watchers in this country, for a compact pictorial guide to the identification of ornithological dejecta. It is hoped that this book will go some way towards meeting that need and spawn other guides of a similar nature in the future.

Actual color photographs and paintings of splays play a vital part in this work and we were indeed fortunate as authors that the many birdsplay collectors who sent in their specimens for analysis (usually presented on good quality plastic kitchen wrap), allowed us to record their most typical and significant dejecta for inclusion in this guide.

The splays chosen for this book represent a broad cross-section of avian species found throughout the region. Not all of course, are common roadside splayers; birds of general interest and one or two rarer species have been included for enlightenment, and we hope, inspiration. Batsplay is briefly discussed (to prevent confusion over nocturnal emissions) and the growing popularity of the splay as art also warrants a section. Flight silhouettes are the preferred pictorial reference; field experience indicates that such a brief and fleeting impression is usually all the driver can manage prior to, or just after, splay creation.

With the growth of environmental concern in recent times, the collection and study of splays has potential to provide fresh insights into the state of our habitat. In the same way that a doctor is able to gain valuable information by examining his patients' stools, this book will enable the average driver to become more aware that splays can help us determine, not only the health of the bird, but also the health of our environment. To this end, our guide does not concern itself with overly-specialized or detailed analysis of splays, but rather aims to provide the driving public with information on collection and a simple method of identification. It is our sincere hope that everyday road users will now feel encouraged to mail samples to the National Ornithological Dejecta Society, particularly when noting interesting variations from the norm.

We are aware there are those who claim an ability to read more into bird splays, and have followed with interest a growing trend to use them to try and predict future events. However, recent claims that the general collapse of communism, and the Gulf crisis, were accurately foretold by the analysis of Greylag Goose droppings over Greenland, are not well supported.

Peter Hansard, Burton Silver
Berkeley, Calif. 1991

Introduction

While the collection of splays only became really popular with the growth of the environmental movement of the seventies, the study of avian dejecta is, nevertheless, a discipline embracing a long and rich historical tradition.

In Roman times, divination included not only the study of birds' flight patterns as a means of determining the future, but splays too, were carefully considered for their prophetic significance.

A green splay on the back of the hand was a sign of future wealth. A red splay foretold illness affecting that part of the body which had been struck. Yellow splays were seen as a sign of great success, while purple splays were the unwelcome heralds of defeat in battle.

The ancient Greeks believed that dejecta striking prospective marriage partners simultaneously was most propitious. Indeed this sign was seen as doubly significant when the dark solids within the splay fell on the male, and the white watery parts on the female. Remnants of this belief are, of course, echoed today in the form of wedding attire; the groom is traditionally clad in black, while the bride wears white.

However it was in China, that the relationship between a bird's dietary intake and the consistency and color of the splay was first established. The price of a caged bird was determined not only by the healthy bloom and rich coloring of its feathers, but also by the beauty and tone of its droppings. It was the fabled Mong Kok Chinese who discovered that feeding robins a diet of agapanthus seeds, tung oil and clit beetles, produced splays with a nucleus of an unusually deep turquoise, and an outer envelope which dried to a vivid blue at the extremities. The bird-sellers of Yung Shue Wan on the other hand, were famous for the scarlet and gold droppings of their nightingales, said to have been obtained by the use of a secret diet which may have included grape skins and tumeric. Deeply impressed at seeing these in presentation form, Marco Polo wrote, "Bird jewels of red and gold most handsomely adorn their collars and and their cuffs."

But more importantly, it is Captain Xavier Cremment, personal communications officer to Napoleon at the time of the battles of Ulm and Austerlitz (1805), who must be credited with the pioneering research on the relationship between avian dejecta and disease. It was Cremment who first observed that the more exhausted a message-carrying pigeon became, the greener its droppings tended to be. This was a crucial factor when selecting birds to carry important orders from Napoleon to his commanders at the front line. In an eloquent demonstration legendary among splay collectors, Captain Cremment graphically described his discoveries while dining

Postage stamps depicting the splays of two threatened species.

at the Palace of Versailles. Using cream, oysters and creme de menthe, (some accounts claim horseradish sauce and chartreuse), the resourceful captain made twenty different little splays on dark blue dinner plates bearing the gilded Napoleonic Crest. By this method, he was able to explain the gist of his findings in considerable detail. It is said that Napoleon, who had a weak stomach, never ate another oyster. However, that great culinary delicacy, pigeonneau á la sauce verte aux huîtres, (pigeon in green oyster sauce), undoubtedly owes its existence to this historic evening in the year of 1806.

In our own century, interest in avian dejecta has grown rapidly with the use of the automobile and the proliferation of roads that now reach even the most isolated habitats. There are seventeen Ornithological Dejecta Societies in the USA and over thirty in Britain. Canada has twelve Avian Splay Leagues and there are other groups in France, Italy, Australia and New Zealand.

It is a little known fact, that the New Zealand Post Office led the world in 1988, when it issued postage stamps depicting the splays of two threatened species, the North Island Kaka and the Blue Duck. The stamps were intended to help drivers identify these splays so that should they be seen on windshields, they might then be reported to the Department of Conservation particularly if sighted in previously unrecorded habitats. The scheme proved successful; three new colonies of kaka were placed under protection in the first six months.

Similarly, a major Irish breakfast cereal company now plans the inclusion of picture-cards, depicting splays of that country's most endangered birds, in all family packs of bran flakes.

With projects such as these already under way, and with the fast-growing acceptance of ornithological dejecta as art, it seems certain that we are about to witness a worldwide explosion of interest in the collection and study of splays.

Collection

There are over 8,350 species of flying birds and for each of them there are approximately 600 possible dietary combinations. Even when ignoring factors such as seasonal fluctuations, new synthetic foods or insecticides — all of which cause excremental variations — a total of 5,000,000 distinct types of birdsplay may be collected on windshields around the world at any one time.

Windshields are in fact, extremely efficient collecting nets. At just 60 miles per hour the average windshield sweeps a volume of air equal to 594 cubic feet per second. On a 60 mile journey, that's the same as spreading a net of some 396,817 square feet. Or, to put it another way, 100 hours of driving equates with a gigantic windshield nearly 1.5 square miles in area, held aloft for one sixteenth of a second. With such an effective gathering device positioned in front of our eyes, it is easy to see why the growing store of fascinating information about dejecta has led to splay collection becoming a major global pastime.

The two most important factors in the capture and preservation of splays are a collection surface enabling the splay to be easily removed, and proper observance of correct drying times so that the specimen remains intact. Most splay enthusiasts prepare the surface of their windshield by first wiping it down with a damp cloth. A sheet of good quality clear plastic film

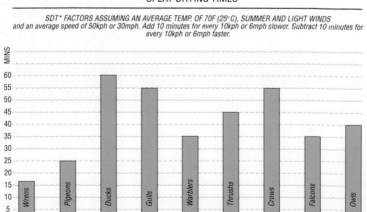

* SPLAY DRYING TIMES

SDT* FACTORS ASSUMING AN AVERAGE TEMP. OF 70F (25°C), SUMMER AND LIGHT WINDS and an average speed of 50kph or 30mph. Add 10 minutes for every 10kph or 6mph slower. Subtract 10 minutes for every 10kph or 6mph faster.

of the clingy type is then laid over the glass. Provided there is some moisture underneath, the film will remain bubble free and sit firmly in place without the need for additional fixing. Once a splay has formed on the surface, it can be easily removed with the specimen *in situ.*

Splays that strike uncovered windshields may be loosened with a clear high-grade oil such as oleander or witch hazel. They can then be carefully removed with a flexible blade. However, this should not be attempted until sufficient drying time has allowed the formation of a binding crust or skak (see glossary). The skak should cover the entire surface of the splay. It is also important to check that the skak is of sufficient consistency to firmly hold larger nucleic particles such as insect debris, seeds, etc. As most drying is achieved by driving which creates an air flow over the specimen, it is necessary to be constantly alert to the danger of losing these more wind-prone pieces and thus significantly lowering the value of the splay.

Drop height, vehicle speed, wind velocity and rain considerably affect drying time. A large, dense, fully-packed and moist splay dropped from a relatively low altitude and striking the windshield of a stationary vehicle will, in the normal course of events, take several hours to dry. Conversely, small splays with a large drop height will flatten and spread over the windshield of a speeding automobile in much thinner layers. But the thinner the splay, the more likely it is to dry quickly and become brittle; your own judgement will best determine the course of action to be followed. Disintegration due to brittleness can often be prevented; a fine mist spray adaptor fitted to the windshield washers will prove effective. Alternatively, the car may be parked in the shade for several hours. Some collectors keep a small, damp, lightweight cloth handy and gently tape it over the splay when driving in direct sunlight.

In cold conditions, considerably increased drying times can lead to unnatural wind distortion and general splay disfigurement. The vehicle should be driven at low speeds until such time as a good skak is gradually formed. When this has been accomplished, higher speeds will then encourage drying without danger to the integrity of the splay. An S.D.T. chart has been included to indicate the drying times necessary to achieve maximum cohesion and structural strength in most splay categories. Natural fresh air remains the preferred drying method, while use of a hair dryer is always to be avoided as it can easily alter the natural spread and texture of specimens.

The various techniques and methods of preparing and mounting splays for exhibition are too numerous and complex to be dealt with here. There are however, many excellent texts devoted to all aspects of this subject and several are listed in the bibliography.

Gavia immer

Common Loon

Description: A large oily, opaque solid. Sticky to the touch and with a pleasant 'wet-fish' odor when fresh. A lacey outer envelope, and large gritty solids well dispersed within a substantial creamy nucleus.

Food: Fish.

Distribution: Northern North America. Winters south on coastal waters.

Collection: This is not an easy item to obtain. Loons rarely stray from the water's edge as they are clumsy on land. The loud wailing call sounds strangely anguished; few scientists believe that the large dejecta is totally responsible. Drive by lake edges at low speeds.

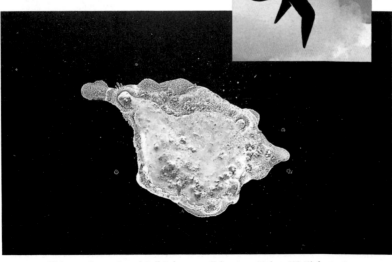

This specimen: Grand Fall Lake, near Princeton, Maine. US Highway 1.
September 12th, 1985. NE winds. 2:30pm. 20 MPH.

mm 10 20 30 40 50 60 70 80 90

Pelicanus erythrorhynchos

American White Pelican

Description: Large, splashing, loose and forceful. A very confident splay, creamy, fishy and acrid. Large envelope shows little nucleus but rather, copious well-dispersed oily solids.

Food: Fish.

Distribution: Northwest, migrating through prairie states to Gulf Coast.

Collection: Pelicans always feed in flocks so multiple splays are possible, particularly during April/May when the breeding season is at its height and there is much display activity. Pelicans often fly at great heights; if conditions permit and luck is on your side, a migratory splay may cover your windshield.

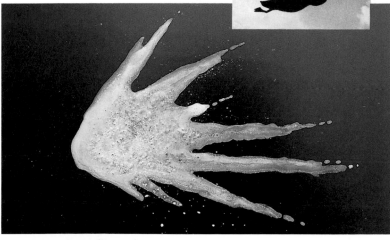

This specimen: Flint Creek Water Park, near Bond, Mississippi. April 15th. 1987. Fresh SE winds. 11.45 am. 35 MPH.

mm 20 40 60 80 100 120 140 160 180

Ardea herodias

Great Blue Heron

Description: A large splay of a generous nature. Wet, fluid and impressive. It is mainly envelopic in that the core nucleus of gritty solids is thinly integrated with the whole. Sometimes vibrant green flecks will enliven the nucleus. Low-flying birds will produce more heavily impastoed dejecta.

Food: Fish, amphibians, molluscs.

Distribution: On both coasts of USA and in southern Canada in summer.

Collection: One of the rarer splays, most often collected during early morning or evenings, along roads in close proximity to water. A speed in excess of 40 MPH will ensure an even spread and good resolution.

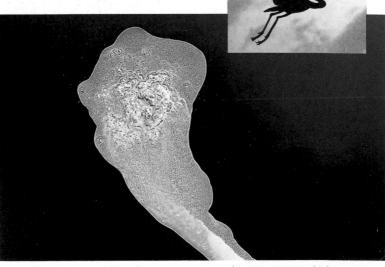

This specimen: Colville Lake, near Sprague, Washington. Interstate highway 90. August 21st, 1984. Fair. Light winds

Branta canadensis

Canada Goose

Description: Copious and sticky, very typical goose dejecta. Little envelope, mostly a greenish solid nucleus the texture of thick glue. When fresh, the powerful 'spinach soup' odor is characteristic.

Food: Water vegetation, some small water animals, pasture, grain, crops.

Distribution: Canada, northen USA, successfully expanding range southwards.

Collection: Vigorous horn honking may alert feeding birds, causing them to rise in startled flight by the roadside. In this situation, there is every possibility of obtaining multiple splays. Open ground or marshy expanses seem to be the preferred habitat.

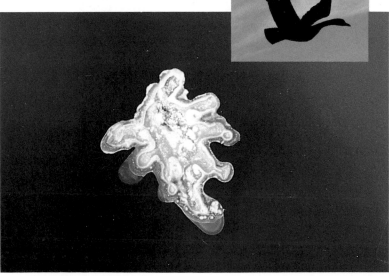

This specimen: Near Dismal Swamp Canal, off Highway 17, West Virginia. July 30th, 1986. Rain. NE winds. 10:15am. 45 MPH.

mm 20 40 60 80 100 120 140 160 180

Cygnus columbianus

Whistling Swan

Description: A graceful, semi-solid dejecta comprised almost entirely of nucleic matter (digested vegetable fibers). Splay envelopes are minimal and in some specimens are missing altogether. Duck-like, but larger envelope.

Food: Mostly aquatic plant life, grains, occasional water insects.

Distribution: Breeds in Arctic tundra areas, winters on bays in more temperate zones.

Collection: Prudent collectors will be aware that high-speed swan splays, though spectacular, may result in windshield coverage of an opacity and spread likely to affect road safety. Road speeds therefore, should always be governed by circumstance.

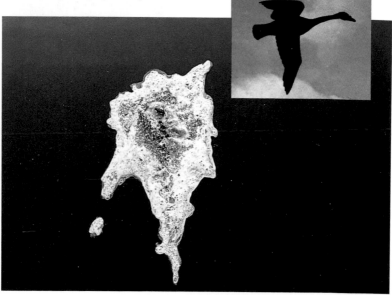

This specimen: Near Scranton, North Carolina. State Highway 264. December 19th, 1989. 12:15pm. 30 MPH.

Anas platyrhynchos
Mallard

Description: A fine, cohesive splay, moist and full with little envelopic spread. Most typically, a creamy green-gray dejecta, displaying the satisfying texture of oil paint freshly squeezed from the tube.

Food: Aquatic plants of all descriptions, grains, water insects, small shellfish.

Distribution: Common. In the north and Canada, this duck prefers western areas.

Collection: Splays are relatively common and best collected at slow speeds on roads adjacent to inland waterways. Dual splays are often taken in the mating season and provide an excellent opportunity for comparative study.

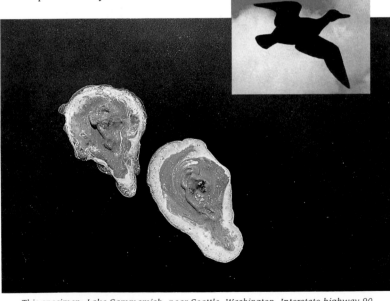

This specimen: Lake Sammamish, near Seattle, Washington. Interstate highway 90. November 11th, 1987. Overcast. Light SE winds. 2:30pm. 5 MPH.

mm 10 20 30 40 50 60 70 80 90

Anas discors

Blue-Winged Teal

Description: Pert and perky. A fairly opaque and reasonably solid dejecta with little envelope and, as is the case with most ducks, a thick sticky texture, with those much prized yellow and purple tints embellishing the overall greenish-gray hue.

Food: Water invertebrates, seeds, etc., gained by 'dabbling'.

Distribution: Southern Canada across to South Carolina in winter.

Collection: A small marsh duck, so try roads through habitats of this nature for best results. Though this duck is diminutive, the dejecta can often be of similar size to that of larger species. As the scientific name implies, this is a splay which will engender considerable discussion.

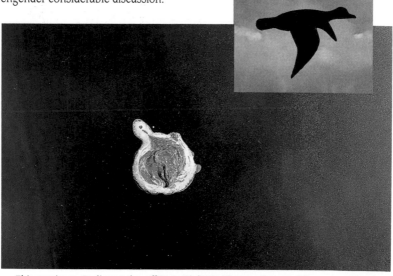

This specimen: Perlican Lake, off State Highway 53, near Cusson, Minnesota, July 5th. 1986. Calm, overcast. 9:25am. 5 MPH.

Cathartes aura

Turkey Vulture

Description: Messy and generous, with a definite tendency to splood. The thick, creamy envelope sometimes contains solids of a bilious yellow (partially digested gristle and fat) that add a sprightly dash of color to the splay.

Food: Carrion. An accomplished scavenger.

Distribution: Southern Canada, right across United Sates to the Caribbean. Some western populations migrate south.

Collection: Desert, grasslands, farmyards and forests are all likely habitats. Look for the 'V' shaped silhouette circling high in the sky. Moderate speeds and sudden horn honking, sufficient to lift birds from carrion, are recognized field tactics. A parked vehicle with carrion attached will also give excellent results.

This specimen: Sonora (near the Caverns), Texas, off highway 290, June 2nd, 1984. Fine and clear. 11:30am 30MPH.

mm 20 40 60 80 100 120 140 160 180

Buteo jamaicensis
Red-Tailed Hawk

Description: A splay which always shows a gratifying response to drop height. The limey envelope has the consistency of paste. The nucleus will be varied, depending on diet, and can show as a dark syrupy brown, diluting down to light ochers and greens. The splay most popularly collected is a typically vigorous white splash.

Food: Rodents (rats and mice), reptiles, insects.

Distribution: North and central America. Caribbean. Widespread throughout, and found over a variety of habitats.

Collection: As this broad-winged, round-tailed buteo may be seen in the vicinity of woodlands and farms, roads in these areas offer excellent possibilities for collection. Fast speeds and high drop height produce spectacular results.

This specimen: Klamath Falls, Oregon, off interstate Highway 97. October 7th 1987, Bright and clear. Moderate NE winds. 10am. 55 MPH.

Falco peregrinus

Peregrine Falcon

Description: Like all falcons, has a streaky splay forming a series of long sploodish streaks (falcon droppings simply fall from the cloaca — whereas hawks eject their dejecta in powerful squirts). White and limey. Variation limited, but look for green subnucleic 'freckles' during breeding seasons.

Food: Mainly small birds

Distribution: Widespread but nowhere common. Breeds on northern cliffs.

Collection: Popularly known as the duck hawk, the peregrine's splay is usually seen near nesting sites or roosts; windshield examples have a rarity value and are much prized by the collector. Coastal, farmland, and high altitude areas are recommended.

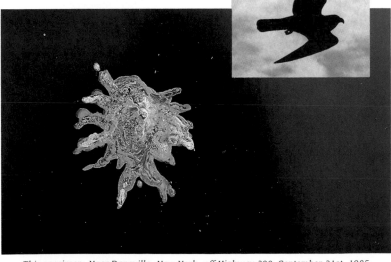

This specimen: Near Dansville, New York, off Highway 390. September 21st, 1985. Brisk N winds. Cloudy. 3:15pm. 45 MPH.

Colinus virginianus

Bobwhite

Description: In fact, a delightful little white 'bob'. Fairly solid and often containing a marbled nucleus the shape and texture of a tiny berry. This is a tight, dry splay, usually forming the classic sklop.

Food: Seeds, fruit, (grasses, shrubs). Crops, (corn, etc.).

Distribution: Widespread in central and eastern USA.

Collection: This small quail (8½"-10½") congregates in coveys which, when not feeding, tend to shelter in a tight defensive circle looking outwards. Some collectors use dogs to flush them out, but this practice is frowned upon by serious splaymen.

This specimen: Near Paintsville, Kentucky, off Highway 23. October 14th, 1989.
Winds from the E. Fine. 12:20pm. 35 MPH.

Phasianus colchicus

Pheasant

Description: Generous and wet with a tendency to splood. A viscous nucleus tends to spread its large fruity solids broadly within the envelope. Warm tonings in fall are indicative of the availability of nuts, berries, etc..

Food: Opportunistic — seeds, grain, insects, small animals.

Distribution: Northern and central USA with expanding population drifts elsewhere.

Collection: The introduced pheasant has colonized agricultural and wooded areas and is a popular game bird; during the shooting season, browsing birds often congregate near open roads, where guns are not normally discharged — in this simple way, the collector can enjoy the game season without requiring a licence.

This specimen: Near Chamberlain, South Dakota. Off Interstate Highway 90.
October 27th, 1985. Cloudy. Calm. 3:00pm. 40 MPH.

mm 10 20 30 40 50 60 70 80 90

Fulica americana

American Coot

Description: Fluid, oily, stringy. A weak envelope surrounds the loose, greenish core. This splay is normally a schplerter with a multiplicity of detached lobes. In the finest examples, these form even more extended lobular patterns (splays within splays).

Food: Aquatic plants and insects.

Distribution: Southern Canada and south to southern states, with some groups wintering in Florida.

Collection: Surprisingly strong flyers, coots are found on lakes, bays and open water, as well as in the expected swamp and river habitats. Speeds should be moderate to prevent complete deformation of the splay. May respond to sudden horn blowing — as splaymen always say, "It pays to toot a coot."

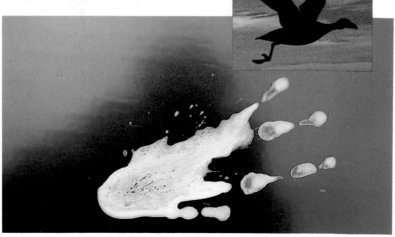

This specimen: Horseshoe Lake, near Bruins, Arkansas, off Highway 38. August 12th, 1986. Light S winds. Cloud. 10:30am. 25 MPH.

mm	10	20	30	40	50	60	70	80	90

Charadrius vociferus

Killdeer

Description: Wet and earthy upon release but rapidly drying to a brittle 'pie crust' consistency. Envelope and nucleus often merge on impact. The schplutz form is typical. Look for sandy soil fragmentation within the nucleus and intricate starburst patterns in the outer envelope.

Food: Soil animals, insects, etc.

Distribution: Southern Canada to central Mexico.

Collection: This large, noisy, banded plover can be found in plowed fields and pasture lands. Head for farmland during plowtime, roll your window down and raising your voice to its highest register, imitate the constant and vociferous call, 'kill-dee!' Speeds are best kept moderate to preserve splay form.

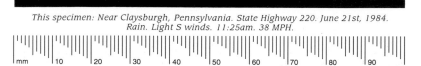

This specimen: Near Claysburgh, Pennsylvania. State Highway 220. June 21st, 1984. Rain. Light S winds. 11:25am. 38 MPH.

Scolopax minor

American Woodcock

Description: Earthy and fibrous nucleus merging with a dull and somber envelopic outer. A splay most generally of the schplutz type. However, barely detached lobes sometimes qualify it as a conservative form of schplerter.

Food: Soil animals.

Distribution: Northern Florida and southern Louisiana up to southern Canada.

Collection: Broadleaf and coniferous woodlands, and their marshes, are preferred habitats. Motorcycles with windshields and four-wheel-drive vehicles are an advantage, though normal roads in this kind of environment offer possibilities.

This specimen: Near Appomattox Natural History Park, off State Highway 131, West Virginia. October 2nd, 1990. Cloudy. SW winds. 12:30pm. 35 MPH.

mm 10 20 30 40 50 60 70 80 90

Larus agentatus

Herring Gull

Description: A large, white limeaceous splay of surprising density and volume. The very large nucleus varies in color and texture according to diet, and will range from a dramatic dark and gritty solid to a paste or gruel featuring delicate shades of cream.

Food: Indiscriminate: fish, fish scraps, shellfish, crabs, mice, eggs, insects, bread.

Distribution: Widespread. Moving into northern latitudes (Canada and Alaska) in summer. Winters near coastal areas.

Collection: Herring gull splays are readily collected in the parking lots of fast-food outlets and on roads surrounding garbage dumps. At the seashore, splaying can be encouraged by tossing bread scraps into the air in the vicinity of the vehicle. Multiple splays are common.

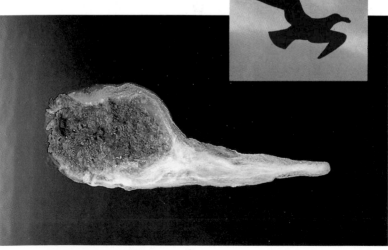

This specimen: White's Landing,(near Lake Erie) Ohio. US Highway 6. August l0th, 1987. Rain. Light N winds. 3pm. 25 MPH.

Sterna hirundo

Common Tern

Description: A splood. Summery, light, precise; as neat as the bird itself. Splays are medium-sized, white, with a sooty nucleic core. Look for occasional green pigmentation of subnucleic solids in the breeding season.

Food: Small fish and insects.

Distribution: In central and eastern USA, a summer breeder. Winters south of Florida.

Collection: Roads near beachfronts, estuaries, lakesides, or island coastlines in summer. All offer the collector opportunities for satisfying splays.
Responds dramatically to high speed impacts.

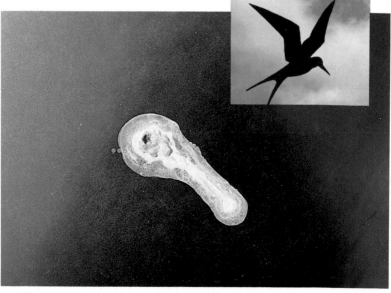

This specimen: Near Arnesen, Lake of the Woods, North Minnesota. June 25th, 1988.
Fine. Brisk N breezes. 4:15pm. 15 MPH.

mm 10 20 30 40 50 60 70 80 90

Columba livia

Feral Pigeon

Description: A generous schplutz with green, brown and, occasionally yellow nuclear material, tending to be well spread inside the somewhat loose envelope. dries to a hard and brittle consistency.

Food: Scraps, spillage, such leftovers as humanity may endow.

Distribution: Widespread in parks and streets of cities and towns.

Collection: Feral pigeon splays should not be brushed aside just because of their abundance. While having no 'rarity' value, splays can be easily taken by driving round and round inner city parks and offer wide scope for comparative study.

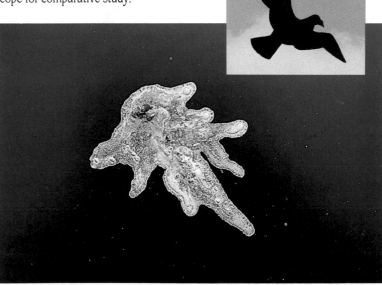

This specimen: 23rd Street, Santa Monica, California. November 1st, 1986.
Fine. Calm. 10am. 30 MPH.

Zenaidura macroura

Mourning Dove

Description: A typical schplutz. Soft and fruity, loose and wet. Mainly envelopic with clear distinctions between outer and inner envelopes. Well defined nucleus often contains large undigested solids.

Food: Grains, seeds, small invertebrates.

Distribution: Widespread from Alaska, southern Canada to Central America.

Collection: This commom wild dove is often shot in numbers and the enthusiastic collector may achieve spectacular results when accompanying a shooting party for the day; drive on roads and trails as close as possible to the guns. Multiple splays are then common; however, dejecta often has greater fluidity than normal.

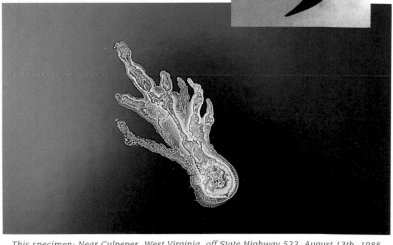

This specimen: Near Culpeper, West Virginia, off State Highway 522. August 13th, 1988. Changeable. Breezes from the NE. 9:45am. 48 MPH.

Geococcyx californicus

Road-Runner

Description: Very runny. A long and streaky slash — a kind of extended splood. Contains a nucleus of gray solids liberally sprinkled with green and rufous flecks. Seasonal tonings have been observed.

Food: Gophers, mice, lizards. scorpions, small rattlesnakes, etc.

Distribution: Western USA, east to Louisiana, south to Mexico.

Collection: As this large cuckoo prefers to run rather than fly, collection can be difficult. Vigorous use of the horn may help it rise. Birds accidently struck by an automobile and which splay on the windshield as they glance off the hood, are legitimate.

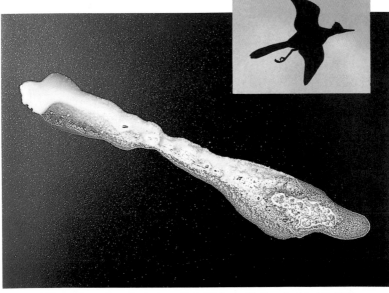

This specimen: Near Contact, on State Highway 93, Nevada. July 1st, 1986.
Hot. Light E winds. 10:15am. 60 MPH.

Tyto alba
Barn Owl

Description: A globular splash prone to considerable lobular extension upon impact. Fascinatingly bland as skeletal and fur remnants of prey are largely regurgitated in the form of 'pellets' (of no real interest to the splayman) without passing through the intestinal tract.

Food: Mainly rodents, large insects.

Distribution: Widespread across USA.

Collection: Crepuscular and later driving near rural buildings, churches, etc. recommended. Birds appear ghostly white in headlamps. When parked at night, roll down your window and try imitating this owl's call: a strangled shriek or an eerie, rasping hiss.

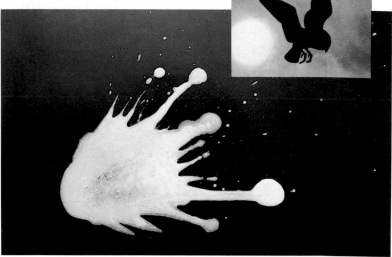

This specimen: Near Clinton, Missouri, Highway 7. Fine and calm. August 2nd, 1986. 9:15pm. 45 M.P.H

Bubo virginianus
Great Horned Owl

Description: A generous squirt of a splay. Streaky white and limey with little nucleic core differentiation (see Barn owl, ref. 'pellets'). An influx of any one particular prey species in an owl's territory may affect the overall color and tonings of the white splay and result in a riotous splash of exuberant ivory-creams.

Food: Insects, mammals, birds.

Distribution: Widespread across USA. Absent from tundra in Canada.

Collection: This large and powerful owl can often be seen when driving through woodland areas at night. Try keeping headlamps dimmed while driving at speed. Parking under a suitable tree with the lights off may prove to be an interesting and wise method of collection.

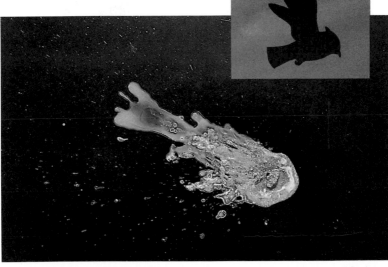

This specimen: Near Glendive, Montana, off Interstate Highway 94. Fine and fresh.
S breezes. September 15th, 1986. 10:40pm. 55 MPH.

Chordeiles minor

Common Nighthawk

Description: A medium to small splay. Dejecta ejected on occasions from a height of one hundred feet or more. The copious creamy envelope contains a handsome brown nucleus giving ample evidence of the insectivorous diet. Because of drop height, often thinly spread in a sunburst pattern.

Food: Flying insects.

Distribution: Southern Canada and much of the United States.

Collection: Forest roads in early evening bring the best results though good splays are occasionally obtained in cities. A slow speed will ensure continuity of spread while mantaining a solid core.

This specimen: Devil's Lake, North Dakota. US Highway 2. August 30th, 1984.
Fine and calm. 8:40pm. 45 MPH.

Chaetura pelagica
Chimney Swift

Description: Small, sooty, not always seen in natural rounded sklop form as drop height is often considerable. Interesting darker solids in the nucleus unmistakably point to an insectivorous diet.

Food: Flying insects.

Distribution: Breeds from southeast Canada down to Gulf Coast.

Collection: Late afternoon and early evening before dark are good times for collection; swifts will be noted busily feeding on the wing while rapidly circling high-rise buildings, houses, treetops etc. Slow speeds are best.

This specimen: Near Wooster, Ohio, off Highway 302. May 12th, 1985. Fresh N winds. (time unrecorded) 45 MPH.

Archilochus colubris

Ruby-Throated Hummingbird

Description: More of a speck than a splay, but a huge asset to the collection of any serious student of ornithological dejecta. Surprisingly well formed with little or no nucleus. Magnification reveals a delicate thread-like aura — the splay collector's 'pearl'.

Food: Nectar and minute insects.

Distribution: Summer breeding visitor. This tiny bird (only 3 inches long) flies as far north as Alberta and Nova Scotia and winters in Central America.

Collection: One of North America's most desirable splays, it responds well to collection on plastic film spread over the windshield. This allows for detailed examination under a microscope at a later time when it can be distinguished from flattened mosquito bodies which it can often resemble. Roads in woodland areas are best and a very slow speed is advisable to prevent disintegration.

This specimen: The Glades Drive, near Vicksburg, Mississippi. May 16th, 1988. Bright sunshine. Calm. 9am. 10 MPH.

mm | 10 | 20 | 30 | 40 | 50 | 60 | 70 | 80 | 90

Megaceryle alcyon

Belted Kingfisher

Description: A wet and rather oily splood of average size. The thick creamy envelope contains a weak yet subtly toned nucleus. A versatile diet allows for considerable variation in this much prized if somewhat odoriferous splay.

Food: Fish, frogs, insect, small snakes, some rodents.

Distribution: North America. Breeds S. Labrador down to Gulf of Mexico.

Collection: Roads alongside streams, ponds and marshes are all likely spots when searching for this large kingfisher. Listen for its loud 'dry, rattling' cry. Parked vehicles may enjoy the most success.

This specimen: Coralville Lake, off Highway 382, Iowa. July 20th, 1985.
Scattered showers. Light NW winds. 2:30pm. Stationary vehicle.

Picoides villosus

Hairy Woodpecker

Description: A small sklop of tightly packed consistency and firm, round contours. Clearly defined inner and outer envelopes surrounding a loose nucleus. Check for exoskeletal remnants.

Food: Surface and sub-surface tree insects, etc.

Distribution: Alaska, Canada, and south to Central America.

Collection: The machine gun sound of a woodpecker drumming in the woods will alert you to its whereabouts. Proceed slowly, keep engine noise low and watch for birds on tree trunks. Continual reversing then moving forward will, over a period of time, help the birds become accustomed to your presence.

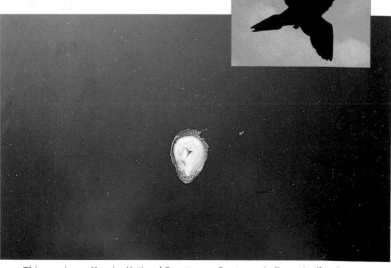

This specimen: Hoosier National Forest, near Freetown, Indiana. April 10th, 1987. Fine, cold. Winds from N. lpm. 20 MPH.

Tyrannus tyrannus

Eastern Kingbird

Description: The so-called 'doily' splay. A medium to small sklop betraying signs of an insectivorous diet. The dark and compact nucleus is nicely encircled by an envelope with the intricate patterns of a white lace doily.

Food: Mostly flying insects, occasionally earthworms and berries, making for varietal dejecta of a rarer and highly collectible nature.

Distribution: Breeds southern Canada, northern USA to Gulf of Mexico.

Collection: This flycatcher is typically seen on fenceposts in pasture areas. Highly aggressive towards other birds, so dual splays can often be obtained while driving through habitat during a territorial dispute or at the beginning of the breeding season.

This specimen: Near Looxahoma, Mississippi by State Highway 4. July 7th, 1985. Dull. Windy from SE. 10:30am. 30 MPH.

Hirundo rustica

Barn Swallow

Description: Small, pert, sklopic. The experienced eye will immediately detect signs of an insectivorous diet. Cream and chocolate blend harmoniously at the junction of the intermediary envelope.

Food: Small flying insects.

Distribution: Widespread. Southern Canada to the north of southern States.

Collection: These swallows nest in all manner of man-made buildings, ceaselessly flying back and forth during daylight hours. Overhead wires offer an additional source of splays; remember, the courteous splayman will always show consideration for other motorists and adjust speeds according to the flow of traffic.

This specimen: Near Pawtucket, Rhode Island. Off Interstate Highway 95. June 9th, 1987. Dull and changeable. Winds from SE. 3:10pm. 43 MPH.

mm 10 20 30 40 50 60 70 80 90

Progne subis

Purple Martin

Description: A typical insectivorous sklop. Examples showing clean separation of inner and outer envelope (uncontaminated by gritty solids) are most prized. Nucleus is dark and mottled and often has a curled 'meringue-like' topping.

Food: Flying insects.

Distribution: Widespread from southern Canada to the Gulf.

Collection: Many bird lovers install nest boxes for use by this popular summer visitor, always closely associated with human settlement. Purple martins can be seen at most times of the day; look for any expanse of water or grass (pools, sports fields etc.) as these are likely insect hunting sites, and attract the bird in some numbers.

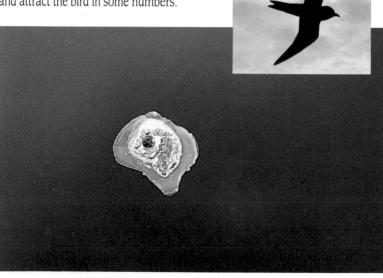

This specimen: Norwich, Highway 2, Connecticut. June 11th, 1987.
Showers. Light E winds. 11:45am 40 MPH.

Troglodytes aedon
House Wren

Description: A small but perfectly formed splay of creamish hue, nicely accentuated by its envelopic encapsulation of frothy cream. Tiny, but pleasantly sculptural in form and always a delight to the eye. Look for expressive solids of an insectivorous nature.

Food: Mostly insects.

Distribution: After wintering in the southern USA (and Mexico) spreads across to Texas and north as far as southern Canada during summer.

Collection: Low speeds along roads in well-gardened suburban areas give the best results. A common splay most often obtained in the late afternoon prior to roosting.

This specimen: Plaisted Road, St George, South Carolina. April 22nd, 1989.
Light showers. Calm. 4:30pm. 15 MPH.

Mimus polyglottus

Mockingbird

Description: A rather loosely formed schplutz. The creamy textured splay is often garnished with bright streaks and flecks (seasonal fruits and berries). Solids suggesting an invertebrate intake are invariably found floating in the nucleus.

Food: Fruit, berries, invertebrates.

Distribution: Southern Canada, across to the Gulf and Caribbean.

Collection: As this is the state bird for no less than five states, a good splay will be an essential item for many collectors. However, the powers of mimicry attributed to this bird extend to splays mimicking catbird dejecta; be sure of identification. In Feb/March the mockingbird is on the hunt for nesting material; string, wool and twigs decorating your automobile may attract attention.

This specimen: Kent, Ohio. Off Highway 59. August 2nd,. 1988.
Bright sunshine. Calm. 2:15pm. 50 MPH.

mm 10 20 30 40 50 60 70 80 90

Turdus migratorius

American Robin

Description: An extended sklop with an attractive cloud-like appearance. Moist, loose, fragile. The nucleus lacks the ability to retain even small gritty solids, which tend to spread throughout the envelope.

Food: Earthworms, snails, insects, fruit.

Distribution: Widespread, common and well known in USA.

Collection: Parks, gardens, woodlands — all offer the collector ample scope. Often seen on lawns looking for worms and a common visitor to bird tables. If wishing to collect locally, simply keep circling the block very slowly. (Should you arouse suspicion in the neighborhood and the police arrive, be sure to check the windshield of their patrol car too.)

This specimen: Bridgeton, Highway 49, New Jersey. July 8th, 1989.
Fine, cold. Winds from E. 2pm. 5 MPH.

Parus atricapillus

Black-Capped Chickadee

Description: A tight little schplerter that rewards the collector with excellent examples of starbursting, even from low drop heights. Close examination may reveal evidence of an insectivorous diet.

Food: Insects.

Distribution: Alaska, Canada, south to central USA.

Collection: These little critters (of the same genus as European 'tits') head for the woods in summer, so wintertime is often your best bet for splays. Chickadees will, at this time, arrive in gardens etc, in groups. With a feeding station handy, splays may easily be taken in your driveway by driving slowly backwards and forwards.

This specimen: Oil City, Pennsylvania. Off Highway 62. November 13th, 1988. Cold and clear. Calm. 1:05pm. 33 MPH.

Cardinalis cardinalis

Cardinal

Description: A small, compact, mainly envelopic splutz, which at times can be brightly colored. Often a sticky, transparent residue replaces the normal secondary envelope. Check nucleus for signs of undigested seeds or insect material.

Food: Insects, seeds, blossoms, buds etc.

Distribution: Southeast Canada. East, central, southwest USA.

Collection: Because the world of splay collection thrives on order and synchronicity, any cardinal splays of a roseate hue are highly collectible. However, food dyes added to bird food will automatically disqualify the exhibitor when detected by routine NODS spectroanalysis.

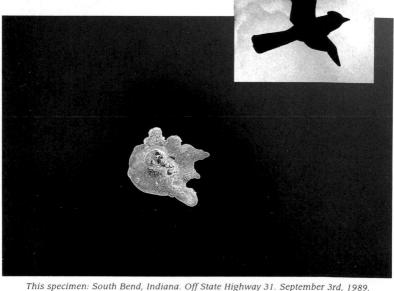

This specimen: South Bend, Indiana. Off State Highway 31. September 3rd, 1989. Dull. Gusts from NE. 12:30pm. 45 MPH.

Passerina ciris

Painted Bunting

Description: Small, sometimes only the size of a grain of rice. The coiled, rather gaudy and squishy nucleus is delightfully encapsulated in a semi-opaque, frothy envelope.

Food: Predominately a seedeater.

Distribution: Breeding range from lower North Carolina, northern Mississippi, central Arkansas, southern Kansas and the Gulf States.

Collection: Drive past garden areas, railway embankments and wastelands when weeds are seeding etc. Expect low drop height. This tight little sklop usually tolerates a wide variety of driving conditions.

This specimen: Twin Pines Drive, Macon, Georgia. June 15th,. 1987.
Light rain. Calm. 12:10pm. 40 MPH.

Passer domesticus

House Sparrow

Description: Small but cheekily extrovert in nature. Nucleus usually a turbulent mix of gray and brown. The porridgey gray and cream envelope is prone to extravagant starburst formations.

Food: Anything going (bread etc.) but mainly grains and weed seeds.

Distribution: Resident. Widespread. Common.

Collection: Hamburger buns can be used as an effective enticement. Birds feeding on fast-food debris (frenchfries, hot dogs, etc.) often display a slight saffron tinting to the otherwise subfuscus palette. Tried popcorn on the hood? Some NODS members would not approve, but it is visually very effective!

This specimen: Outside Tom Bradley Terminal, Los Angeles International Airport, California. August 16th, 1990. Fine and calm. 7am. Speed unrecorded.

Sturnus vulgaris

Starling

Description: Med-small. A sploshy splotch of a splay. Thick white envelope with a juicy nucleus, sometimes vulgar because pretentious. Will radiate dramatically on impact to form thin, semi-opaque, often bubbly starburst showing much lobular extension. A true schplerter when speed and drop height are favorable.

Food: Soil insects, worms, spiders, snails, slugs. Also seeds, berries and fruits in season.

Distribution: Resident. Widespread and common.

Collection: One could spend a lifetime delving into the intricacies of starling splays alone. A wide range of dietary substances, combined with seasonal variations, make for everchanging splay factors. If lucky enough to park under a communal roost, the splay enthusiast will be richly rewarded.

This specimen: Phil's Wood, Berkeley, Calif. Overcast and Calm. November 5th, 1989. Stationary vehicle (no time recorded).

Cyanocitta cristata

Blue Jay

Description: A medium-sized splay, generally splashing in a manner befitting such a raucous and aggressive bird. White and limey envelope. A varied nucleus, usually brownish-gray, but some attractive yellows or even orange, tones may be present if fruit or berries are in season.

Food: Virtually omnivorous, Jays will eat insects, slugs, worms, fruit, berries and the young and eggs of other species.

Distribution: East of the Rockies.

Collection: In recent years this splay has beem most successfully collected on the visors of helmets worn by trailbikers frequenting wooded country normally inaccessible to the average automobile.

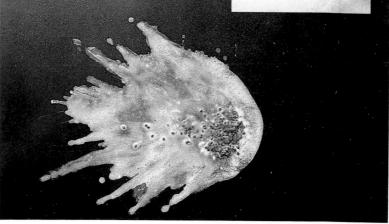

This specimen: Near Clarksburg, West Virginia. Gilbery Forest Park, Route 9. November 5th, 1989. Changeable. Blustery SW gusts. 2:30pm. 10 MPH.

Corvus brachyrhynchos

American Crow

Description: A confident, medium-large splay comprised of a thin, loose, pasty envelope with a pronounced tendency to spread and streak. Often, no nucleus is visible. Sometimes a neutrally toned and partially digested solid will enliven the otherwise bland 'whitewash' effect.

Food: Omnivorous: farmyard chickens, carrion, small rodents, grain, foliage and insects in quantity.

Distribution: Widespread from southern Canada to New Mexico.

Collection: Those unconcerned with accurate nucleic preservation (not always an essential factor in Corvidae exhibits) can enjoy a liberated approach to collection. With a relatively high drop height, a stiff head wind, and speeds of up to 80 MPH, magnificent splays of up to four feet across are entirely possible. Rain helps achieve greater spread.

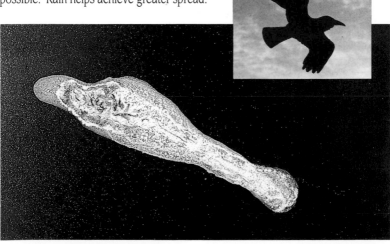

This specimen: New York, NY. Central Park. March 16th, 1990.
Showery, Light NE winds. 4pm. 30 MPH.

Bat Splay
A short note on the Chiroptera

Although bats are the only mammal that can actually fly, their dejecta is usually of little real significance or interest because unlike avian splays, it lacks an outer envelope and is comprised of an unpleasant and cohesive monochrome nucleus, decidedly 'mousey' in smell, and with little real potential for graphic starbursting of exhibition quality.

'Large aerial mouse-droppings' might at first seem to be an apt description, but batsplays can sometimes be remarkably fluid and sticky. No doubt slight tonal variations and a shift in fecal hue can occur, but without the contrast of a splashing white envelope, so readily and happily associated in our minds with birdsplays, there is generally little to fire, or even capture, the imagination.

An exception could perhaps be made in the case of the three species of Vampires, all of which are New World fauna. After feeding on the blood of cattle or mules, they return to their colonies and produce amazingly pungent and syrupy dejecta of a rich, streaky brown.

The flight silhouette given here, seeks to represent the typical sighting, and is included purely to help avoid confusion with bird species sometimes seen hawking for insects at dusk (swifts, swallows, martins. etc.). As a splay forming on the windshield at night cannot always be presumed to have come from a species of owl or some other night flying bird (gulls and migrating species often fly great distances on clear nights), it follows therefore, that occasionally, bats will be responsible.

Hopefully, by using the guidelines mentioned above (lack of envelope, 'mousey' smell, etc), such dejecta can safely be identified and destroyed forthwith.

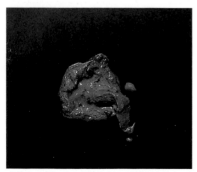

The splay of the Common Short-nosed Fruit Bat,
Cynopterus marginatus

A dual splay of the Common Blood Sucking Vampire,
Desmodus rufus

The Splay as Art

Interest in well-framed specimens of avian dejecta is hardly confined to those of an ornithological persuasion. In recent years, the splay has gained increasing attention within the established art community. Mounted splays both real and artificial, while admittedly still a controversial element of the art scene, are beginning to command high prices. A dual splay of the Blue Winged Teal, dated 1983, was sold recently in a leading Dallas gallery for $6000. Similar prices for top quality compositions have been obtained in London's Cork Street. This trend comes as a surprise to the many who question whether splays can truly be works of art.

There are two major schools of thought on this. On the one hand, there are those who simply see the splay as falling within the broad context of found art. This method allows that art is what an artist says it is, and that if a splay collector says his exhibit is art, then so it is. On the other hand, there are those led by David Hinds, Curator of the Department of Arts, University of Bristol, England, who see the splay as having an important place in what has become known as the Green Movement. This movement, sometimes called Behavioral Art, has strong links with abstract expressionism, and its leading exponent, Jackson Pollock, created many famous splay-like compositions curiously reminiscent of areas surrounding large communal roosts.

Abstract expressionists shunned the idea of producing purely representational images and instead, expressed themselves by the manner in which they applied paint to canvas. It could be rolled, poured, brushed, smeared, trickled or thrown. The crucial thing was that the feeling that lay behind the doing of the work had to be communicated within the final image. David Hinds argues that, "the mounted and framed dejecta of a bird is not excrement in the artistic sense, but rather an expressively applied image. When you look at a splay you will immediately recognize the manner in which it was cast down. In precisely the same way, you can immediately recognize how Pollock felt when he applied paint to canvas. You can sense a forceful or irritated expulsion in some dejecta, just as you might sense that certain other splays have been released gently with a feeling of quiet relief. So by viewing a splay in an artistic context, you achieve greater empathy with the bird itself...even the most insensitive people feel differently about a little bitty brown sparrow poop compared to the huge creamy white splash from a low flying cormorant."

Essentially, the Green Movement views the splay as a viable artistic message, one that apart from telling us what the bird in question may have been eating, allows us to get in touch with a particular bird's feelings. In the early nineties, the movement has gone even further with artists such as Busch and Rewi in Ireland, and Hillary and Holden in America, attempting a much deeper involvement with the bird by imitating its excremental method.

Application is by two rubber tubes joined together to represent the ureter or cloaca found at the posterior end of the bird's alimentary tract. Each is filled with a paint substitute for the urate (white,liquid) and fecal (dark, solid) splay components, then held high above the canvas. The artist often prefers to adopt an avian posture while meditating in a bird-like state. Some painters flap their arms and even emit chirping sounds. At the precise moment of greatest excremental empathy, the tubes are squeezed, sometimes with actual buttock pressure, and a 'splay' is formed on the canvas.

No matter how experimental an art form seems to be, no matter what medium is used or what movement or school it claims to belong to, the basic criteria that make for art always remain the same. These criteria are: structure, form, composition and integrity; without these, critics agree, no old master or modern abstract painting can be taken seriously. How then does the splay measure up to these criteria?

The splay has structure because it is solidly based on dynamic geometric principles. It is forced by muscular spasm and intestinal dimensions into a structural whole. The splay has form too, because the interplay between dark and light tones prevents it from looking entirely flat. The texture, the wonderful chiaroscuro emanating from the interaction between envelope and nucleus, suggests technique, style and above all, visual reality.

It is in the area of composition that splays sometimes fail as art. Usually this occurs when the exhibit is mounted and framed in a way that disregards the 'Golden Rule'. This dictates an exterior proportion of any size proportionately equivalent to thirteen feet by eighteen feet, (portrait or landscape) but insists on extra width at the bottom of the mount so that the whole is naturally pleasing to the eye. When this convention is properly observed the splay is immediately brought within the realms of true art.

Finally, integrity. We need be in no doubt in this regard; one only has to look at a splay to realize it was 'meant'.

Rewi's *'Spasm'* on show at the Natural Image Gallery in Dublin.

Acknowledgements

Planning, research, writing and photography for this guide have taken the best part of three years to complete. We are deeply indebted to the many people who have given so generously of their time and knowledge during this period.

Special thanks is gladly given to the many dedicated members of Ornithological Dejecta Societies (on both sides of the Atlantic), who so willingly assisted with the collection and photography of splays. Without their help and encouragement, this book could not have been produced.

We owe a great debt to the president of the National Ornithological Dejecta Society of America, Bob Brockie, who in the last year alone, traveled more than 6000 miles in order to determine the exact splay drying times for species included in this edition. Also Erena Rutherford and Astrid Malcolm whose splay reconstruction work has been of inestimable value. Working non-stop over a three month period, this dedicated pair successfully rebuilt the rarely obtained splay of a Common Loon, *Gavia immer,* from nearly two thousand tiny dry fragments.

We are grateful to Graham McMahon who supplied detailed information on methods of determining splay consistency prior to their transfer, and to Ashley Conland who generously shared information on swept volume, capture time and the blur factor, from his own research papers prior to publication.

We also acknowledge our debt to Dr Pat Norris, whose analysis of genuine splays found in cabinets of early taxidermy has been invaluable. And we would certainly fail in our duty if we did not express our appreciation of the outstanding collection work of Captain Nick Dryden. A typical example of the dedication he has shown over the last three years is illustrated by the removal of the wheelhouse window aboard his trawler during atrocious conditions in the southern Pacific Ocean. The window had been struck by a six foot wide splay of a Wandering Albatross, *Diomedea exulans,* and was, remarkably, returned to harbor intact.

But our greatest single debt is to Heather Busch who devoted two years of her time, without remuneration, to extensive travel in the British Isles, Europe and North America. Photographing splays in conditions that proved extremely trying, Heather's VW van had to be shared with three dogs, two cats and a parrot. Thank you Heather, Floyd, Oddy, Sod, Lixy, Lozenge and Bigbit.

P.II. & B.S.

Glossary

APR Avian Preference Ranking. Refers to the relative likelihood of a surface being covered by a splay. The windshield of a moving vehicle has a high APR as does the top of the head.

audibon Soft sound made by avian dejecta as it strikes a windshield and forms a splay. Audi (l) sound, bon (fr) good, literally, good sound.

avian Of the bird kind.

bogor Dry or semi-dry splay, broken into pieces during an attempt at removal from the original surface. A bogor may be reassembled and glued to another surface, but it always remains a bogor.

chewits Dried flakes of splay which collect along the upper surface of windshield wiper blades and gives the impression that the rubber has been chewed. Chewits may also find their way into the air intake vents below the windshield, and create an interesting miniature snowstorm effect throughout the vehicle when the ventilation fan is first turned on.

clap-trapping Use of loud clapping or horn blowing to startle birds into low flight defecation in the vicinity of a surface designed to trap the resultant splay. The use of this technique, while effective, is frowned upon by some British dejecta societies.

capture time Time taken for dejecta to fall the depth of a windshield. Depends on drop height, depth of windshield and speed of vehicle. Dejecta ejected at 100 feet, in the vicinity of a vehicle with a 1.5 foot high windshield, traveling at 60 M.P.H., would have a capture time of one sixteenth of a second.

constellation Group of splays with many tiny associated star like splatter specks giving the appearance of the night sky.

dejecta Excrement.

dooby Incomplete or partial splay caused by dejecta breaking up prior to being formed into a splay. Doobies are usually the result of high winds or telegraph wires. Not to be confused with a fooze (q.v.). Low collection value.

drop height Height from which dejecta is ejected. One Ruppel's Griffon Vulture splay had a recorded drop height of seven miles.

dual splay Two dejecta from two different birds of the same species, forming splays adjacent to each other at the same time. High collection value. (Triple splays are very rare). See also horlop.

envelope Exterior container of splay containing uric acid. Usually white.

exoskeletal Bony or leathery external structure e.g. insect wing casings, etc.

flarks (also skrits or skrittles, UK) Sharp gritty particles sometimes found in the nucleus of a splay, which may scratch the windshield if dragged across it by the wiper blades.

fillmilner Windshield almost completely covered with splay matter. The result usually indicates an excellent days collection or one cormorant.

fooze Splay completely disfigured by impact with windshield. Usually due to excessive vehicle speed, high winds, or poor splay consistency. No collection value.

garl Unique tangy smell produced by the rapid drying of a splay on a hot car hood. The presence of a garl is a sure sign that drying is too rapid and will result in an overly brittle specimen.

goony Dried nucleus representing the only visible remains of a splay, usually resulting from the white envelope having been washed away by rain. Goonies are collectible and often mounted with pins on heavy card.

horlop Splay made up of several droppings from different birds. On many occasions a perfectly good splay may become a horlop when partially or totally covered by another. Horlops have little collection value but are of increasing artistic interest, due to their exciting blend of colors and textures.

insectivorous Of insects.

koote Splay that restricts vision and needs to be removed before driving.

lobe Pendulous extension of splay wall.

NODS National Ornithological Dejecta Society.

nucleus Solid core of splay containing fecal material.

ornithology Study of birds.

pav Semi-solid, mainly envelopic splay that dries rapidly with a pointy meringue-like skak (q.v.).

schplerter Large splay with multiple or detatched lobes.

schplutz Variable sized splay with extended lobes.

skak Crust forming over the top of a partially dry splay. Attempts to remove a splay from its original surface usually result in a bogor (q.v.) unless a skak has formed over the entire surface.

sklidder Dejecta containing a large solid object, such as a berry stone, that skips across the windshield leaving several splays in a straight line.

sklop Small splay. *See* Splay Topography.

splay Avian dejecta containing both fecal and urate portions, formed in a spread out manner, after ejection from a height onto a hard surface. Also known as a 'spread' in Ireland, a 'whitey' in Australia, and a 'bolger'- in New Zealand. Also, v. to splay on, ie, to eject dejecta that forms a splay.

splayman Person who collects and studies splays.

splerd Large splay, mostly envelopic.

sploober Flexible plastic tube used to suck up a wet splay and transfer it to another surface.

splood Splay of variable size with a single extended lobe.

SDT Splay Drying Time.

Bibliography

BIGGS, I.T. *Identifying and Removing Splays from Solar Panels and Umbrellas.* Journal of the Minnesota Avian Dejecta Society, Vol.1, No.2, 1987.

BENTON, H.,and ROSS, R. *Happy Days with Jay Splays. A Practical Guide for Pre-schoolers.* San Francisco: Tricycle Press, 1990.

CRICHTON, A. *The Chinese Hat Method of Splay Collection.* Journal of the Lamma Avian Dejecta Society. Vol.2, No.1, 1990.

DARWIN, C. *On the Origin of Faeces.* Unpublished Manuscript and Public Lecture, Albert Hall, London, 1869.

GARRICK, R.,and PYE, W. *The Effects of Low Temperature on Splay Viscosity and Drying Time.* Journal of The Canadian Avian Dejecta League. Vol.1, No.2, 1991.

HYDE, N.O. *Creative Embellishment in the Fossil Splays of Archaeopteryx and the Pterosaurs.* Ph.D.diss., Victoria Univ., Wellington, N.Z, 1990.

McMAHON, G. *How to Read a Whitey.* Darwin: Newmarlick Press, 1971.

MALANE, D. *The Splay and Abstract Expressionism.* Ph.D.diss., Wedde Univ.Col., Toronto, 1989.

PETTIGREW, J.P. *Winter Splays. A Skier's Goggle Guide.* Chicago: Fairview Press, 1976.

PRIOR, P. *Hygroscopicity as a Factor in the Formation of Structural Defects in Avian Dejecta.* Am. Nat. 123: 967-991, 1986.

ROSE, C.N. *Proceedings of the Second International Workshop on the Creation of Artificial Splays.* University of Tokyo Press, Tokyo, 1991.

SAINSBURY, M. *Fifty Favorite Frugivore Splays.* Dublin: Scatta Press, 1984.

SCOTT, T. *The Use of Avian Excremental Material in Tibetan Divination Ritual.* Smithsonian Institute, Washington DC, 1990.

UNWIN, M. *Splay Money. 101 Creative Ways to Exhibit and Market Ornithological Dejecta in America.* New York: Fox Books, 1989.

WHERRY, A. *Making Big Spreads. Preparing, Photographing and Blowing Up Splays in Ireland.* Feakle: Bloom Books, 1985.

WILSON, Q. Ornithological Dejecta. Its Automorphic Significance in the Green Movement. *Encyclopedia of American Art*, New York: Simon and Putnam, 1987.